other than they seem

Tupelo Press Snowbound Chapbook Award Winners

Barbara Tran, In the Mynah Bird's Own Words
Selected by Robert Wrigley

David Hernandez, *A House Waiting for Music*
Selected by Ray Gonzalez

Mark Yakich, *The Making of Collateral Beauty*
Selected by Mary Ruefle

Joy Katz, *The Garden Room*
Selected by Lisa Russ Spaar

Cecilia Woloch, *Narcissus*
Selected by Marie Howe

John Cross, *staring at the animal*
Selected by Gillian Conoley

Stacey Waite, *the lake has no saint*
Selected by Dana Levin

Brandon Som, *Babel's Moon*
Selected by Aimee Nezhukumatathil

Kathleen Jesme, *Meridian*
Selected by Patricia Fargnoli

Anna George Meek, *Engraved*
Selected by Ellen Doré Watson

Deborah Flanagan, *Or, Gone*
Selected by Christopher Buckley

Chad Parmenter, *Weston's Unsent Letters to Modotti*
Selected by Kathleen Jesme

Allan Peterson, *Other Than They Seem*
Selected by Ruth Ellen Kocher

otherthantheyseem

Allan Peterson

T|P

Tupelo Press
North Adams, Massachusetts

ISBN: 978-1-936797-84-4

Cover and text designed in Plantin by Bill Kuch.
Cover photograph: "Feather" (2012) by Allan Peterson. Used with permission.

First paperback edition: November 2016.

Tupelo Press
P.O. Box 1767, North Adams, Massachusetts 01247
Telephone: (413) 664–9611 / editor@tupelopress.org / www.tupelopress.org

Tupelo Press is an award-winning independent literary press that publishes fine
fiction, nonfiction, and poetry in books that are a joy to hold as well as read.
Tupelo Press is a registered 501(c)(3) nonprofit organization, and we rely
on public support to carry out our mission of publishing extraordinary work
that may be outside the realm of the large commercial publishers. Financial
donations are welcome and are tax deductible.

"Treasure your exceptions"

—William Bateson

Contents

Other Than They Seem

TASK

A tug is passing like a cake of lights
push boat plowing the whole night
otherwise there was nothing
to indicate it could be passed through at all
or be solid enough to hold up the house
me having my shoulder to the door
a task both oblivious and difficult
my deltoid and dream-stained sheets exhausted

HEARTS

I am not touching my hand to my heart

that is too dark

I am touching the shirt pocket with my pen

where my hearts are

one above the other   One a hollow muscle

an accessible learner

then a pen light storing words like a battery

so when written they will have light to read by

METAPHOR

I do not like the step ladder
Not for the frightening heights
but sorrow has a heat that rises
and each rung echoes the stifling
silent strata of lost lives
Below sorrow it is so cold
and distant it might be Michigan
where for three months it hurts to talk

LONGING

Point to the longing they said and I touched a map

of the whole body

the ulnar   radial   that which draws tears

from fingers after touch

the words soothing and lying at the same time

cloudburst   sunrise

a whiteness like a bone and then your picture

NO TELLING

These words have changed so often
there is no telling
what was said or how it came to this
I remember mentioning bees
the efficiencies of lightning   language trying
to say what the brain looked like
convoluted with a sunset at one end
I remember time passing and hearing
little ticks of it all over the house
occasionally a faint bell
the touch of a brushstroke to transfix the hills
hints of a small hoof on flagstone

ILLUMINATIONS

Having winters more severe
there was the problem of constant accrual
how to bury the dead
Charnels full   the earth already frozen
and littered with stones
in desperation they began loading the oceans
I have been trying to place them to paper
but nothing fills there   memory takes no space
Even assembled together
my lettered illuminations might be no more
than flashlights behind the moon

UNDER COVER

The yellow bird sits on on my finger
It can talk but only at a third grade level
I say the capital of North Dakota
It wants to change the subject   cuttlebone
is suggested to keep its beak keen edged
I had no such eloquence   I was still
in the second reading group at school
wondering why we even had two Dakotas
The bird was certain heaven was a cloth
I knew it as a book between the sheets

PROCESS OF CULTURE

A dustpan beginning as a hand
sweeping crumbs of one thing into another
becomes eventually a tooled silver flatness
with a handle in the shape of a bird's wing
brothered by a whisk
Culture is a distance between you
and your hot meat antecedents
A fork for eating instead of your fingers
A hand on a cat that left a mouse on your shoe

GONE

When that bird is gone we cannot speak of it

and the words once given us are gone

and we are not forgiven

When it is missing it is still us to blame

and we remember in the middle of a sentence

apropos of nothing being spoken

a sweet sweet   sweet sweet

the very sentiments we once thought to save us

LIMITATIONS

We can hardly accomplish anything

straight out   even explanation can't shortcut mystery

and make the world simple as lies

after all we know about complexity

So we try it the hard way

theater and film   poetry and fresco

little glass rods that can be twisted into horses

ATMOSPHERE

When I saw the sunset all the blue

had drained out of Nevada

the slow tree with the thin years in it

an empress in vermillion chiffon

drifting down behind the Sierras

After an epiphany or scare

one feels histamine tingle skin

I remember beauty is self inflicted

On a gridded floor I watched a spider

choose a path that graphed optimism

A pale moon rose like a ghost of soap

AVAILABLE LIGHT

Last night we sat passive in a dark room

a hematite sky accompanied by music

Large figures who lived in available light

loved and failed against one wall

When the lights revived hours later

the survivors that valued the dark gathered coats

the stars of their nightmares rolling behind

CATEGORY 2

The instructive part of weather was "feels like"

hence the primacy of sensation over thermostats

Now something alphabetical is up to "I"

whirling offshore hugely famous with itself

and there was temperature and time

dressed like Thursday in a loose grey suit

a natural mechanism where at intervals

a door opens and a small wet figure strikes a bell

AGING

is one thing we do without practice

Our breaths wing beats just to stay aloft

Little speed ups convince me

there is a bird that visits my heart

with the same flutters others have described

But this is my heart my bird

I feel its wings when it practices

learning to fly to the willow with my hair

IMPACTS

As a hatch of black flies hints at an infantry

a platoon scouts me now

young females ready for blood called by life

as I am to smack them flat

fast as lightning struck the oak in Beulah

The three horses under it

now lie dead on their sides their eyes open

focused behind us on a long thought

PRACTICAL PURPOSES

This morning a small wire jumped in my hand
I thought *first dorsal interosseous*
like seeing quickly a flick in shrubbery
and thinking redstart   thrush
And when a tight banner cable snapped
I thought how long bones might
shatter like broom straws raving into pain
But since we recover
from so many indignities   even arrogance
I thought this spasm will pass
needing maybe hypnosis   a little potassium

INNOCENCE

The lights were on in its one brown eye

Half the sky was in the heavens

the rest in lakes and puddles

It was not auspicious

The buck was up with me at five

lying with its look that the eaten ivy

had nothing to do with him

just coincidence a relaxed face

saying innocence followed by a line of zeros

TOMORROW

Tomorrow will be partly cloudy
The other part will be buzzing
and small collisions
a bird on the crossroads sign
a song above a plus
Weed Eaters will answer each other
throughout the valley   bees will dance
every sound will proclaim itself
better than silence
I will leave a few letters out of my voice
horses will turn blue before the hills
then I will make a pet of sleep

NOT JUST AN APPLE

Not just an apple   a whole limb

falls in the side yard loaded

some streaked fruit

some green party lights

The problem is interpretation

It looks like mortality to me

but I am falling behind already

still working to understand

the bird with burned shoulders

angels in the alcoves turned to stone

TRANSMIGRATION

Watching the sky and the backyard

I look up confusing fall warblers

And they are   but so are the sparrows

and regional peeps and some Canadas

one of eleven varieties starting with a "v"

changing travel into wavering script

People among us think they are spirits

passed out of dead bodies   It's possible

I know my own lost voice can enter a wire

in Providence and emerge in California

home of the the Marbled Murrelet

DISPLACEMENT

We live in bodies we still are vague about
This morning my shoulder spoke
while lifting the woofer a slipknot of thorns
where the clavicle meets the acromion
musical names attending the pain of discovery
I felt the house and footsteps   the truck outside
whose idles shook the door   the weight pulling
springs and straps together the most flexible
joint in the body but subject to displacement
I remember yesterday like it was tomorrow

I HAD BEEN SPEECHLESS

just thinking of making English out of birdsong
I had been merging star charts and paint splatters
counting petals so they ended on loves me
saying wasps for the hint of a secret like pssst
and   as if illustrating the identity of specificity
and paraphrase   there came Orion then a killdeer
walking in from the dock like a normal person

HEIST

With the sky fairly smothered
I cannot see how brush marks make a chair
or a tree of feathers
how dreams go in and out of me like a breath
with music holding up the room
or land forms in a mile going foothills to flat
the light brushed off each evening
as I do dirt the driveway or finally midnight
passing before the clock
holding up its thin surrendering black hands

WRITING LIFE

Speech is all over everything like dust

and if not saved

is swept away easily with a cloth

or like silver utensils tarnishing silently

in a padded box

of aromatic cedar lid closing with a click

The latent world wavers between us

By closing one eye we can make the furniture shift

and we can do it to the moon

NOTHING AFTER ALL

When the inexhaustible is gone
infinite whittled down to finite measures
gaps and voids packed as cactus
and when we don't have a word for it
death will do
When memory's a hum of static
when the retrospect is present
and zero will be nothing after all
half the heart waiting for contraction
scarce as usable troubles
history would be like living in a house
without a dictionary

MEANING

The split moon is fulfilling its deal with darkness
how much to give up how often and how long
to become the face on the waters looking back at itself
So what is meant is a little beyond the words
and next to them and under as shadow as something
they give off themselves the shadow's shadow
that is the nothing but what it is and nothing after

Acknowledgments

Poems from this book previously appeared in the following journals:

"Atmosphere" in *Ladowich* Magazine

"Available Light" in *ForPoetry.com*

"Category 2" in *Cascadia Review*

"Displacement," "Gone," "Longing," and "Tomorrow" in *The Weary Blues* (Ireland)

"Hearts" and "Practical Purposes" in *Poetry Bay*

"Heist" in *Barnstorm*

"Limitations" in *The Seventh Quarry* (Wales)

"Meaning" in *Verse*

"Metaphor" and "Process of Culture" in *Short Poem*

"No Telling" in *Prime Number*

"Not Just an Apple" in *Memorious*

"Task" in *Girls with Insurance*

Some poems may appear here in slightly different forms.

Other books from Tupelo Press

Fasting for Ramadan: Notes from a Spiritual Practice (memoir), Kazim Ali
Another English: Anglophone Poems from Around the World (anthology),
    edited by Catherine Barnett and Tiphanie Yanique
Pulp Sonnets (poems, with drawings by Amin Mansouri), Tony Barnstone
Moonbook and Sunbook (poems), Willis Barnstone
gentlessness (poems), Dan Beachy-Quick
Personal Science (poems), Lillian-Yvonne Bertram
Brownwood (poems), Lawrence Bridges
Everything Broken Up Dances (poems), James Byrne
Hammer with No Master (poems), René Char, translated by Nancy Naomi Carlson
New Cathay: Contemporary Chinese Poetry (anthology), edited by Ming Di
Calazaza's Delicious Dereliction (poems), Suzanne Dracius,
    translated by Nancy Naomi Carlson
Gossip and Metaphysics: Russian Modernist Poetry and Prose (anthology),
    edited by Katie Farris, Ilya Kaminsky, and Valzhyna Mort
Entwined: Three Lyric Sequences (poems), Carol Frost
Poverty Creek Journal (lyric memoir), Thomas Gardner
My Immaculate Assassin (novel), David Huddle
Darktown Follies (poems), Amaud Jamaul Johnson
Dancing in Odessa (poems), Ilya Kaminsky
A God in the House: Poets Talk About Faith (anthology),
    edited by Ilya Kaminsky and Katherine Towler
*Third Voice (*poems), Ruth Ellen Kocher
Yes Thorn (poems), Amy Munson
Canto General: Song of the Americas (poems), Pablo Neruda,
    translated by Mariela Griffor
Lucky Fish (poems), Aimee Nezhukumatathil
The Ladder (poems), Alan Michael Parker
Ex-Voto (poems), Adélia Prado, translated by Ellen Doré Watson
Mistaking Each Other for Ghosts (poems), Lawrence Raab
Intimate: An American Family Photo Album (hybrid memoir), Paisley Rekdal
Wintering (poems), Megan Snyder-Camp
Swallowing the Sea (essays), Lee Upton
Lantern Puzzle (poems), Ye Chun

See our complete list at www.tupelopress.org